How to Face Unemployment

How to Face Unemployment

A Road Map to Success

"Attitude is a very little thing that makes a big difference"

Albert Weil

authorHOUSE®

AuthorHouse™
1663 Liberty Drive
Bloomington, IN 47403
www.authorhouse.com
Phone: 1-800-839-8640

Published by AuthorHouse   08/27/2012

ISBN: 978-1-4685-2382-9 (sc)
ISBN: 978-1-4685-2383-6 (e)

Library of Congress Control Number: 2011961915

Any people depicted in stock imagery provided by Thinkstock are models, and such images are being used for illustrative purposes only.
Certain stock imagery © Thinkstock.

This book is printed on acid-free paper.

Because of the dynamic nature of the Internet, any web addresses or links contained in this book may have changed since publication and may no longer be valid. The views expressed in this work are solely those of the author and do not necessarily reflect the views of the publisher, and the publisher hereby disclaims any responsibility for them.

Contents

ACKNOWLEDGMENTS:

I decided to write this book to help people during a very difficult moment of their lives. Most of the tips included in the text are based upon my own personal experience. After a very successful career I was laid off due to circumstances completely beyond my control. All of the sudden I was, for the first time in my life, facing an uncertain future. Honestly, I did not know what to do or where to begin, I felt lost and scared. I wish someone could have given me advice and support, but when looking around I was alone. Beside the typical personal comforting comments and best wishes I did not receive any specific advice. Well this book is, in a way, my contribution to all people that need a guide to help finding a new job.

Prologue

When I lost my job, for the first time I was not receiving offers of employment and I urgently needed to find one. At first I felt ashamed and guilty. I asked myself, "What have I done wrong?"

I didn't want to share my feelings with friends and family, and certainly not my fears. How could a successful executive all of the sudden be unemployed?

At the very beginning, I neglected to listen to people who wanted to help me. The uncertainty about my future was a burden heavier than I could bear. I tended to isolate myself from people and even began to distance myself from family and friends.

Finally, I understood that this was just another challenge. I needed to change my attitude. It was not like in the past, when companies knocked at my door to offer me a job. I now had to be more proactive, aggressive, swallow my pride and walk a path I had never walked before.

I decided to write this book to help millions of people who are currently unemployed, and whose lifestyle is at risk. Yes, it is not only a new job, but it's also your life. Once we understand that, then we have already taken the first step in the right direction.

Transform This Bad Experience Into A Positive One

As unemployed people tend to be over stressed, concerned and worried, they miss the opportunity to enjoy things. Do not do that to yourself. I did it for a long time. I know it is difficult, but you must fight for yourself. Take as much as you can from this experience.

Improve your skills, enjoy your family, organize your life, take time off, but most importantly, stay active in looking for a new job.

Introduction

For most people, their work is an extremely important part of their life. It is their main source of income, and unfortunately we need money to pay our bills. When you lose your job, that feeling of security fades away, exposing you to your deepest concerns.

In addition to that, your routine is modified. You need to create a new dynamic in your life. This is a very challenging situation but you must work on it. It is healthy to build a new routine.

The current labor market situation is extremely volatile. Even employed people start to worry about their own position. Nowadays, securing a job is essential and also difficult. It does not depend solely on the employee's performance, but also on the company in particular and the economy in general.

There are two main tendencies in the market that increase uncertainty.

Employers Tend To Hire Employed People

I do not have a definitive reason for that, but it is true. Perhaps there is a perception that unemployed people must have performed badly. That is not necessarily true, but it will take time to change. Ninety percent of offer letters are addressed to employed people. Not very promising, right?

Another reason could be that to be actively employed allows a better exposure to contacts and markets trends. In sum, you are in the game. The longer you are unemployed the worse it is for you.

Still, employers will review a candidate's work history carefully, because they now have the opportunity to acquire employees with high potential at a lower cost vs. low performer employees at a higher cost. Again, it will take time to materialize this change in the labor market behavior.

The Average Unemployment Time Is Increasing

It will be fair to say that, in the past, the average unemployment time was about three months. New statistics show an increasing unemployment period that is reaching almost 34 weeks on average due to the state of the economy. This period is still shorter than most unemployment programs offered in most countries.

This is particularly alarming in terms of personal finances. The severance package, if any, could end way before a new income is secure. That is why spending habits must be regarded cautiously.

In this book you will find tips that will most certainly help you to overcome one of the most difficult experiences in your life.

Decreased Salary Pressure

The larger available labor supply is causing a decrease in salaries. For instance, MBA graduates from the top ten Universities are now accepting salaries as low as $80K per year in the US, while in the previous cycle; the average was approximately $120K per year.

There are several reasons for this. The most important one, as mentioned before, is higher unemployment rates and a not very promising recovery of the economy in the short term. Additionally, many companies are taking precautionary measures and are hiring high potential candidates at lower pay rates. Remember companies need to increase profitability.

You Might Be The One

Despite the horrible labor market situation you have to think positive. I am very rational as an economist and thought, "Why bother looking for something if the overall situation is so grim." I also thought I would not accept a lower salary, and that I could not accept just any job because that could set back my resume. The institutional prestige, salary, job title, responsibilities and etc., all came to mind. I was so frustrated!!!

Then I started to realize that my other colleagues were finding new jobs. Perhaps it's not the job of their dreams, but a very decent job nonetheless. There are always possibilities on the market. Crisis always brings opportunities.

My most important recommendation is the following; do not feel intimidated by the market situation and keep on moving. You just might be the lucky one!!!

You Are Not the Only One

The first reaction after receiving the news of being terminated is often rage. After a few days, you start to understand the reality of your new status. At some point in time, when the job-search process begins, you may feel rejected and disliked. Moreover, you may feel ashamed.

The first thing you must understand is that it is probably not your fault, and you are not the only one who is unemployed. You should not feel self-pity or despair. Help yourself, and accept other people's help as well.

The last couple of decades were characterized by impressive growth of productivity, which increased companies' profitability, and it was reflected by good performance of the stock market. Nevertheless, deep macroeconomic changes produced several waves of layoffs in different industries. As a result, millions of people were affected in the process.

Some of the most important causes that generate unemployment are:

- The Privatization Process
- The Consolidation Process
- The Globalization Process
- The Internet Meltdown
- The Technological Shock
- The Over-Leveraged Economy

Let's analyze each one of them.

The Privatization Process

In the past, federal or local governments owned most utility companies. By the eighties, the highly inefficient public companies needed to change to private ownership and management.

The privatization process was particularly promoted by Ronald Reagan under whom the term "Reaganomics" was born. Prime Minister Margaret Thatcher adopted the same concept in the United Kingdom. This process immediately spread out to other European countries and finally to other regions in the world, such as Latin America, almost a decade later.

The utilities sector was the most affected one. Telecommunications, electricity, gas, water, and sewer distributions were particularly active. Transportation, oil upstream and downstream operations also passed from government hands to private ones in a fierce bidding contest.

New operators, after reviewing companies' financial and operational conditions, decided to increase productivity sharply, and a large number of long-term employed personnel were dismissed.

Change was particularly difficult for these people, because in most cases, they were never exposed to private management companies. Their adaptation process was so challenging that most governments launched training programs, and in some cases, employees also received psychological support.

The Consolidation Process

The search for profitability was fueled mostly through the search for economies of scale. This last process was led by M&A (mergers and acquisitions) transactions. Creating a larger corporation could free resources in duplicated areas. As you can probably imagine, it is not necessary to have two human resources, accounting, or administrative departments, as that would be duplicating.

Each merger had not planned to add two plus two equals four. The aftermath should add to at least five in terms of benefits. The difference is the cost reduction of duplicated areas and its impact on the P&L. Of course, that does not only include personnel but also office space, supplies, and marketing expenses, among others.

The last two decades were very active in M&A activities. The banking, telecommunications, and food industries were the most affected.

The Globalization Process

The globalization process, also led by M&A transactions, adds more pressure to the labor market. In this process, some additional unemployment is created, but not to the same extent where companies with the same geographical coverage merge. In this case, the banking industry was once again very active.

Additionally, with the arrival of new technology companies that are able to centralize activities around the globe such as Back Office, Call Centers, Production Lines, etc are transferring jobs to developing countries from developed countries. The beneficiaries of this process are countries and/or zones with lower labor cost and a less-regulated labor market, or in some cases a better-prepared labor force. The down side is that work positions are minimized in one area and then created in another, causing higher unemployment in the former.

The Internet Meltdown

The rapid upsurge of thousands of Internet ventures in the late '90s financed by eager venture capital funds attracted new executives and employees, making it the fastest-growing industry ever.

Unfortunately, misleading concepts implied in Internet valuations, reckless usage of funds, lower adoption rates than expected, and poor management performance in certain cases brought the inevitable. The companies were shot down at the same speed that they had appeared previously.

The interesting thing is that the consequences of this crisis, and the downturn of the stock market (most notably the NASDAQ), spilled over into other industries, such as media, advertising, technological infrastructure providers, and real estate, among others.

The reinsertion in a labor market at the verge of a recession was at least challenging. It is the first time in recent history that extremely capable and very well educated workers were then unemployed. The bad news was that the competition for new jobs was fiercer than ever before.

The Technological Shock

The increasing adaptation of technologies in certain functions is a significant threat to employees. The introduction of Enterprise Resources Planned (ERPs), CRM (Customer Relationship Management), etc. produces a lower need for personnel, mostly in the administrative and accounting area. Less affected are employees who handle direct relationships with customers (producers).

New technologies will keep on appearing and it represents a permanent concern. If you think automated programs could replace your work in the future, try to change the focus of your career to less-risky job functions.

Service industries will be severely affected by new technologies. Unfortunately, this industry is very labor-intensive, and the risk is high. Front-end jobs are likely to be the more secure ones.

Another option is to become very aware of the latest technologies. Up-to-date personnel will likely be kept. Always try to be one step ahead of your colleagues, even if that could imply researching after hours. In the long term, it will pay off. You could lower the risk of being terminated, or you could gain a promotion.

The Over-Leveraged Economy

The recovery of the economy after the 2001 economic "recession" caused by the Internet melt down (bullish equity market) and later the September 11th attack was mostly based on a monetary expansion policy.

The monetary expansion led an oversupply of available credit to acquire almost anything, for instance, homes, cars, etc. Lower interest rates in turn led to an unparalleled appreciation of assets, most notably real estate assets. Additionally, the very poor underwriting policies from certain banking institutions and the use of complex financial instruments only exacerbated the inevitable, a major crisis in the financial service and its consequence, the meltdown of the economy.

The "irrational exuberance", so often mentioned by Mr. Greenspan led prices to an unsustainable level and like any other episode of overvaluation the fall is abrupt and far reaching. In this new recession period the most noticeable consequence was the liquidity crunch that affected several industries, since consumption in the US and other developed countries is fueled by consumer credit. Investments in general were also deeply affected by the contraction of financing options and the negative wealth effect (in fact wealth destruction) suffered by the sharp decline of assets. Banking institutions soon realized that the collateral used to secure the loans was not sufficient to cover the loans made. Their financial situation was so grim that only a massive bailout package helped sustaining one of the main pillars of a capitalist economy, the banking system.

The main consequence of all previous events is the generation of more unemployment. In a globalized economy, even unemployment has become an "export" item. The effect of the current crisis extends beyond all national borders and its effects are very vivid in the US, Europe and other areas of the world.

Reassess Your Skills

As it was mentioned in the last chapter, the actual unemployment crisis lies principally on structural changes, however it is also determined by the microeconomic environment and most importantly by personal performance (why was I terminated?).

There are several important questions

Am I Working In The Right Industry?

Some industries are undergoing a very difficult situation. You should ask yourself if it is realistic to find a new job in the same industry or if it's better to change industries. If the latter is the case, then you should plan your strategy carefully.

Am I Working In The Right Geographical Market?

In today's globalized world it is also important to fully understand the current situation and the future direction of your local market. Some local economies or even an entire country's job market situation could have change abruptly or gradually, and new horizons must be considered.

Was I Working In The Right Company?

Sometimes employees are terminated just because the management team of a certain department did not do their job properly and the company went bust. In this case you could pursue searching a job in the same industry.

But the most important question is:

Are My Skills Still Attractive To The Current Labor Market?

It is key to determine what you should do in the future. To have a better understanding of your own situation you could ask your previous employer the reasons for your termination. Sometimes, for political reasons, you will not get a straight answer. In such a case you must find the answer yourself.

If you think you lack a skill in order to increase your chances of getting a new job, then this is time to invest in yourself. Start learning what you are lacking; it could be a language, software knowledge, etc. Fortunately thanks to the Internet, there are hundreds of courses on-line at a low cost (even free).

If you have a comfortable financial situation, you could consider improving your Resume by starting a Masters degree or other post graduate program in the field of your expertise. Do this not only for the knowledge in itself but also for the network you could build.

If you have had an outstanding professional career, only target prestigious colleges and universities. Otherwise, you will set back your resume rather than improving it. If the cost for higher education is too high, apply for one-year executive programs or three-month senior executive programs.

A question that is related with the previous one is:

Is My Previous Role Still Necessary In The Midst Of All These Technological Changes?

New technologies have a direct impact on certain activities. The jobs most affected are the administrative and accounting. If you belong to one of them, then you should to start thinking about changing your profile.

Find Yourself A New Expertise

Try to switch to more front office, technology intensive or organizational activities in the future. Research & development, international divisions and booming sectors (i.e. alternative energies), are some potential areas where finding a job are more likely.

Finding a new expertise could imply the need to acquire a new skill, such as learning new languages, attending professional courses, seminars or post graduate programs, etc. Unfortunately, most of them, and especially the most recognized ones are expensive. This career move will depend upon your interests, skills and opportunities.

Take Advantage Of Resources That Your Employer Offers To Improve Your Skills.

As most companies have advantageous tax incentives when paying tuition fees, take advantage of the company's training programs or courses while you are still there. This will always be welcomed due to the need for highly motivated people.

Of course, if you are unemployed you will need to invest your own money. Try to prevent this situation in the future by maximizing the possibilities your employer would offer.

Your Finances

As soon you are notified of your termination, you must reassess your financial position and capabilities. It is important to redefine your budget by plotting your new cash flow. The first thing you must know is how long you are able to survive without any additional income, using your existing savings. Dividing your current savings amount by your monthly expenses, you can obtain a ratio that represents the number of months you have to find a new job.

Do Not Waste Your Severance Package

The severance package must be carefully used. Do not assume you will have a new job soon. This money is not an invitation to go shopping; it's your insurance. If you are lucky enough, you will be able to spend it when securing your new position.

Rebalance Your Portfolio

This is not the time to have a large stake of your portfolio in equities, even less, options and futures. At this time, cash is king. Capital protection products, money market, short-term notes and bills will best suit your needs.

Prioritize current yield instead of capital appreciation. Normally, interest-bearing securities have less volatility than non-bearing securities. By pursuing this strategy you will accomplish both of the following targets, reducing your risk and generating positive cash flow.

Reassess Your Budget

One of the most important assignments you should perform is having a complete understanding of your expenses. Once you have a complete list of all expenses, evaluate from 1 to 10 the relevancy of each expense on the outflow chart. After detecting irrelevant or dispensable expenses, eliminate them immediately.

If you think for any reason that you will be unemployed for a long time, perhaps you should take greater actions. This may include selling a house and buying a smaller one, or even renting one. Cancel (suspend) club memberships, leisure activities and etc. It is particularly important to be realistic.

As average unemployment is currently estimated at 34 weeks, try to plan for at least six months without income. Doing this, you will probably be on the safe side.

It is important to make all family members understand this new situation. Everybody should be on board. It is not simple, but it is an opportunity to teach your kids the challenges of life. This could be crucial in order to make them understand the importance of education and savings, among other values.

To preserve a good relationship with a spouse, upon this new reality, requires good communication. Make sure to directly express the new priorities and agree to the cost cutting measures. A commitment must exist between both parties. This new experience will challenge your marriage for sure. If you are on the same page it could also be a very positive experience.

Refinance Your Debt

Once the credit institutions know you are unemployed, the probability of obtaining a new loan is drastically reduced. As soon as you are notified or suspect you will no longer be working, consider the following options:

a) Get a Home Equity Line
b) Refinance your Debt
c) Accept other credit lines

If you have a mortgage you must evaluate it to try to increase the length of the loan in order to decrease monthly payments, especially if you are in the later years where payments are composed by capital.

You could also get new credit cards for a rainy day. It is very likely you will never need to use these new credit lines, but it is better to have everything set up from the beginning. Once you are unemployed, the credit market will not be as accessible to you.

Use Government Financial Help

In most countries, the government has plans to help unemployed persons by administering a monthly payment, especially in Europe. Unemployment compensation paid by the government is normally lower than the previous salary earned by the employee when active. This is why is so important to reassess your budget. The length of this help varies tremendously. You must become familiar with all unemployment benefits offered by the government and what are the terms & conditions of this help. Some companies have compressive programs to train laid-off employees in different areas.

Delay Important Decisions Until The Situation Becomes More Stable

During the unemployment period it's not wise to commit to important decisions, such as buying a new house, car, yacht, etc., since this would present you with larger fixed monthly outflows or reduce your capital stock.

Limit The Downside (Risk)

You should try at any cost to limit your risk. This includes losses from your investment portfolio as mentioned before, however it also includes preventing potential liabilities.

If your company was paying for medical or life insurance, try to keep it ongoing (COBRA Program in the US). It is much better to cancel cable TV, than to have an accident and face liabilities that could compromise your liquid assets.

Car insurance should also to be reassessed. It could be better to increase the coverage or decrease the deductible, just in case. When employed, an accident can be paid off, however when unemployed you might lack the funds. Just imagine yourself unemployed and with no transportation.

Have An Exit Strategy

You must be prepared for any scenario. Think carefully about what your possibilities are. Perhaps you built equity on your home. In this case, you must apply for a home equity loan before your credit deteriorates. If you have a car lease, analyze if it is possible to cancel it and buy a cheaper car in cash, etc.

Regarding other possible income sources, it could be time to start a business of your own, or with other people who are in your position. You could pool investments and buy a rental property, open a restaurant, a retail store, etc. Each person will have different skills, hobbies, interests and possibilities. You must decide whether it is a good idea for you or not.

Bear in mind that having a business requires effort, commitment, expertise and organizational skills. If you have these required skills, it may work out for you. Otherwise keep away from it.

Regardless in all cases make sure you minimize the capital requirements needed for the investment, and make sure you have plenty of reserves to fund your personal finances plus the business needs. Otherwise stay out of new ventures. Bear in mind there are some activities that are not cash intensive and could generate income rapidly, such as real estate agent, insurance broker, multilevel marketing, etc.

Your Personal Life

As it was mentioned before, unemployment brings uncertainty, stress and emotional conflicts. All have a direct impact on your personal life.

Increase Communications

Some people feel so depressed and ashamed when they are terminated from employment that they do not even dare to tell their spouses. This is a huge mistake. If the people who surround you do not know what is happening to you then they will not have the chance to help or understand you.

You will very likely be more impatient, anxious, defensive and aloof. Remember this is only a temporary situation. If you explain your concerns, people will be more tolerant with your "unfriendly" attitude.

A lot of marriages fall apart in high stress situations, especially due to money related issues. Do not let that happen to yours. Always remember that it takes years to build something and seconds to destroy it.

Do Things You Were Unable To Do Before

Try to use your new free time to do things you've always wanted to do and never had the chance before. It could be a wonderful experience if you use your time wisely.

How many times have we said, "How I wish I had time to do this or that". Well, this is the time. Seize the opportunity.

Change Your Lifestyle

Change the way you spend your time and money. Move from cash intensive activities (restaurants, movies, opera, ballet, etc.) to time-consuming activities (sports, beach walks, etc.).

The disruption of your current lifestyle trend may cause you frustration, depression or anger. Those are useless feelings. The only thing that will make you feel better is finding a new job or to be in the process of doing so.

You must diminish all areas of conflict. If your personal life is doing well and you manage to organize your finances, you will be able to focus on finding a job. On the other hand, if your attitude begins to hurt your marriage and other areas of your life then you face two problems instead of one. Think twice before doing or saying something you will certainly regret.

Increase Social Activity

At this point you must be open and able to take other people's advice, references, contacts, etc. For this reason, if you are reclusive and remain at home, you will not be helping your situation.

You never know where the help could come from. Every hour of every day, an opportunity could arise. Be open to help.

It could also be important to join networking groups, professional associations, chamber of commerce or any organization having a direct relationship with your industry.

Comfort Your Loved Ones

When was the last time you cooked your spouse a romantic dinner or went to a park with your family? You do not need to spend money to express love.

How many times have you said to yourself, "I wish I could have more time to enjoy my wife and kids". Now you have the time. Take advantage of it.

Visit friends and family that you have not seen in a while. It is helpful to feel loved and be surrounded by people who care about you.

Look Around

Most of the times we are so consumed by our daily routine that we are completely unaware of our surroundings. We walk the streets without enjoying the landscape, architecture, vegetation or even the sky. We do even not know the city that we live in. Go to the museums, the parks and the historical places offered in your city.

Go to places you have never gone before. Walk around and forget the car. That will give you time to think in a lateral way, not encapsulated in your routine.

Rebuild Yourself

During this time, it is VERY important to increase your self-esteem by reading books, cultivating yourself, going to the gym, or starting a diet. This will help you to avoiding frustration and depression. You should try to like yourself. We generate an aura of energy around us and the better you feel the higher are the chances you will attract a new job.

Use Your Time Wisely

You should have different time horizons to achieve different goals. Your daily schedule should include a set up time to find a new job, another to rebuild yourself, a time to be with family and friends, and a time also to organize your files, accounts, etc. It is crucial to find a balance in your life.

It is an ideal time to think about personal projects. If you have enough money you could take a break and take your time to plot a bullet proof strategy. Traveling could be particularly motivational.

Keep Yourself Busy

You have to keep moving. If you stay still and dormant, you will become more depressed. Your self-esteem will be lowered, and you certainly will not find a new job. By exercising, reading, studying and socializing, you will help yourself.

Finding A New Job

To find a new job is a job in itself. In the current market situation it is difficult to find opportunities without effort. I highly recommend setting aside at least 4 hours a day to work on finding a job, at least in what I have called the Active Phase. This phase represents the preparation process followed by the Interactive Phase and lastly the Passive Phase.

Deploy A Strategy

In order to be successful you must have a strategy. This is not the time to leave your future to depend on your luck. You have to think about yourself, your market, prospective employers and marketing materials (Resume, Cover Letter, etc.).

You must define how you are going to distribute marketing materials, whether by e-mail, fax, regular mail, etc and also to which Human Resource managers, head hunters, CEOs, heads of departments, temporary agencies, etc.

You have to prioritize your contacts. Prepare a list of all future prospects and sort them by type of job and kind of contact (main contact, lead to contact, referral contact, etc).

Analyze Yourself

The first thing you must decide is what you would like to do. In this phase, you must evaluate your skills, your financial situation, along with your position and your sector of expertise. Determine if any of these are lucrative or not.

This is an internal process and perhaps the most difficult one. Your most recent experience could play an important role in the decision making process. In this phase you must evaluate your weaknesses and your strengths. The idea is to use your unemployed time to improve your weaknesses.

As we do in business, you could prepare a SWOT (strength, weakness, opportunities and threats) analysis of yourself. The first two are concentrated on internal skills while the second two represent the external environment, or in this particular situation, the industry where you worked and your functions within it.

As an example, there is Mr. X, who was working in the international banking industry.

Strengths: Self-motivated, flexible, cross-cultural experience, languages, broad knowledge of several banking business units and quick learner.

Weaknesses: Not having a specialization. Generalists compete with long-term executives in corporations, which narrow the available positions. Relocation creates a diversified network, but not localized which makes the job search difficult in a specific market.

Assess Your Market

Opportunities: The banking industry is going global, which could imply more international staff requirements.

Threats: The banking industry in undergoing an impressive consolidation process, which frees qualified personnel who compete directly for future openings.

You must also think about your relationship with teammates, superiors and subordinates.

Analyze which job you would like to get and the skill set required to perform the job. If you think you are prepared go for it. On the other hand, if you are not, fill in the gaps by taking proactive steps to get there.

Distribution Strategy

Nowadays, there are several channels you are able to explore to find a new job. The two main channels are One-to Many and One-on-One, each of which have different sub channels.

One-To-Many

When you send your resume to a company and to job-hunting firms, which are in contact with several other companies, this distribution strategy is called one-to-many.

The importance of this type of channel is that you reach a broad base of companies indirectly. Additionally, the response is quicker because when companies use such channels they are actually looking for candidates, thus meaning there is an opening.

The most important one-to-many channels are:

Internet Based Search Firms: The Internet has become an important means to search for employers and employees. The easy accessibility and low cost has transformed the Internet into one of the most cost-effective ways to exploit the labor market, therefore creating a virtual labor marketplace. There are several companies in the market such as Monster.com—(chief Monster for executives), and specific target markets such as LatPro.com for Spanish or Portuguese speakers. The websites can easily be found through search engines or, for instance, at Careerbuilder.com where more than 70 sites are presented.

On these websites you also have support to help prepare your resume, cover letters, etc. One of the major problems is that you have to upload your resume to make it available to readers. In this process you get bored or unable to use the format you desire. Additionally you have to select your keywords carefully; otherwise you will not be selected in the search. Some services include the options to have several keywords (different resume versions or titles). This is particularly important to candidates who have several areas of expertise.

Specialized Search Firms (Head Hunters): Some companies hire (pay up to 33% of the annual compensation) specialized search firms to find new candidates. It is important to understand that they represent the employer. Depending on their seniority or current appointments, they may be willing to interview you.

Present a clear strategy. Stay focused. You cannot say you are willing to accept any job. Recruiters usually need to put a hat on you. This candidate is for "paper & pulp industry", or for a "CFO" position and etc. Recruiters need to narrow your capabilities.

The worst thing you can do is to show them uncertainty, despair or doubts. They are going to introduce you to their client. That is why they want to make sure you are a good candidate.

These head-hunter firms are actively introducing e-business platforms where you can up-load your credentials on-line.

Job Hunters: In this scenario you hire a job hunter to find you a job. There are certain headhunters that act as job hunters as well. You will not be asked to pay anything, however in some cases you will pay them a percentage of your salary for a specific period of time. Remember they represent you. They give you advice and support and they will be actively looking for opportunities that may suit you.

One-to-One

When you send your resume to a target company directly (to which you are applying for a job), the distribution strategy is called one-to-one.

One-to-one, is important because you can personalize your presentation letter. In the best-case scenario you may know someone in the company who could act as "promoter." Or better still is when you know who the decision makers are.

In reality, it is extremely difficult to obtain an interview without a promoter who is on the inside so try to get one through your network.

As it was mentioned before, *Personal Contacts* are your best option in helping you achieve an interview or land a new job. *Referrals* are the second best way to get in the door to an interview. Referrals work when someone you know referred you to someone he knows inside the company. Finally, when you contact someone without any prior knowledge of the person or institution it is known as a *"Cold Call"*.

Once you know which Company / Position you want to target you should identify what is your best way to get an interview by deciding who to contact. Your options are:

Head of Business Line: If you know which department or division you are interested in then you might be able to obtain the name of the head of the division, therefore address the cover letter and resume to that person. This is the most specifically targeted search since that person will most likely be your future boss. In this scenario you could be more detail or technically oriented since this person has a very clear understanding of your capabilities and his needs.

Human Resources Department: When you do not know to whom to address your resume, the safest bet is the human resource department. It is wise to call the company first to get the name of the HR department director. Remember personalization is key for success. HR departments coordinate all the companies' searches and perhaps there is an opening that could fit your profile that you have not thought of. To stand out from a pile of resumes is not easy. In order to make recruiters life easier try to be very clear on your objectives, position, etc.

Institutional Web Sites: Most companies have sections on their website called careers, job opportunities, "join us," etc. that represent a recruiting tool. In some of them you will be able to see current opportunities, while in others you will receive information where to send your resume such as an email or fax number.

News Paper Announcement: This is a great opportunity because you already know there is an opening. However sometimes you do not know the name of the employer (International Leading Bank is looking for XX). In this case, try to understand the job description and the needs of the company in order to prepare your marketing material accordingly (cover letter and resume).

Do not copy the job description. Instead use your experiences and skills to match their expectations. Give examples of your achievements. It is increasingly important to quantify results, for instance: "I managed a team of 5 professionals"; "Under my supervision sales grew by 45% in one year"; "I led the company restructuring plan allowing a 24% cost reduction in the quarterly budget".

On the other hand, if the announcement mentioned the name of the company then it will be much easier to investigate. Learn all you can about the company through its website or through contacts. Customized and tailor the resume and cover letter upon the information you've received.

Preparation Phase (I)

This is one of the most important phases because the success of the following phases depends on the success of the preparation phase.

Once you have determined what you would like to do, then this is time to prepare the marketing materials such as your Resume and Presentation Letter (or cover letter). Additionally, for more senior positions, a slide presentation or business plan could be prepared if thought appropriate.

You could think ahead and get recommendation letters from your ex-employers in advance. Usually, recommendation letters are the last item you will be asked for in the recruitment process. If you have the opportunity to get them in advance, then do so.

Resume

Your resume is a document that states your main academic and professional achievements over the course of your life. It is not an autobiography. Most resumes are thrown away for bad formatting, typos or defective structure. This document will be filed in employers' databases and will be circulated among "head of departments", interested in your profile.

Prepare An Outstanding Resume

The document should be *clear, consistent, simple, brief and focused.* Remember, recruiters receive hundreds of resumes at the same time, and they will only take about a minute (if you are lucky) to look at your document and decide if you are "eligible". If it is too complicated or formatted poorly, it could be eliminated at once regardless of its content.

Your resume is a marketing tool. Target your resume depending on the recipient. Focus on experiences and accomplishments relevant to each potential reader. Each sentence is aimed to sell your skills, strengths or knowledge. If you think that some past experience does not add value to your resume (too old, not relevant enough for the job, etc), shorten it or eliminate it.

Learn The Tips

The structure is key. As the recruiter will dedicate a very short time to review the document, the structure of the document has to be clear. I recommend having at least three columns. The first one should be the dates. The second, the company and the job title held. The last is the location. This data should be readable at a glance. You can highlight these three items by using bold letters and larger fonts. In the second column, below the company and job title, you can include your main responsibilities, achievements and job description. Just below this include at least 3 bullet points with your most important achievements in this job assignment.

Make it readable: Avoid articles and pronouns (I, me, my, the, an, a, etc.). The resume is a form of business communication. Change from "I developed the marketing strategy" to "developed marketing strategy."

When stating the facts you could use bullet points or narrate them. Use ones that best present your work experience and results. You could describe your responsibilities (narrative style) and outline with bullet points your most important contribution.

Avoid technical words: Most of the recruiters from the human resources department are not prepared to understand technicalities. If they find the resume too complicated you could be eliminated. However if you send the resume to a unit head you will need to be more specific.

Use power words: It is crucial to use the right wording. Prioritize active verbs. For instance: Led, Developed, Implemented, Coordinated, Launched, etc., instead of passive verbs, "responsible for", or "duties include", etc. Use adjectives for emphasis: strong growth, successfully introduced, etc.

Quantify Results: Once again emphasize your accomplishments and support your statements. "Developed new marketing strategy resulting in 47 new clients in 12 months", instead of "Increased Client Base." The latter is an empty statement and too general. Or instead of "Responsible for recruiting" you should try: "Hired 20 staff members."

Remember that some information is confidential so be careful not to breach any confidentiality clause from your previous employer. In this situation rephrase the statement: "Increased client base by 51% in nine months." By using percentages instead of figures you can easily avoid this problem.

Introduce magnitudes: It is important to give an idea of magnitude. This could be done by quantifying amounts (in monetary figures or percentages), in terms of time frame (accomplishes the goal in one year, or accomplished daily deadlines successfully, etc.), or in terms of money (*"saved* 40% on production process", *"earned* USD 250 thousands by . . .", *"managed* 50M budget per year", etc.). Numbers are powerful marketing tools if used correctly. Remember this.

PAR Methodology: An effective way to introduce your accomplishments is to present the problems or challenges you faced, which actions you took, and finally what were the results of your actions. This methodology is called PAR (Problem, Action, Result). You can also present the result first and the problem at the end. Some examples are: Problem: low margins—"implemented cost restructuring and hired new top sales forces, resulting in 34% margin increased." Or you could state it the other way around: "Increased 34% margins, by hiring a new top sales force and restructuring cost structure."

Keywords: New technologies are used to search resumes in databases. Many sorts or searches are conducted through keywords. These keywords are different among industries, companies, etc. One way to determine the right keywords is to read several announcements or job descriptions posted on the Internet for that industry or company. The use of keywords should be used not only as a title, but also sprinkled throughout the resume.

What Is The Appropriate Length?

There was a tendency in the past to make resumes lengthy, so lengthy in fact, that no one read them. As a reaction to this, the market determined that one-page resumes were the solution.

Today, the view on the appropriate length of the resume has changed. We are reaching a balance where ***relevant content*** is the most important driver to determine the resume length. It also depends on experience, industry, objective, education, number of employers, accomplishments, etc.

Nevertheless there are a few hints that might be useful to you.

If you have less than 10 years experience consider a one-page resume. If you have several positions with the same employer, or want to change the focus of your career, your past experience is not that relevant. In such a scenario a one page resume could be the right choice.

If you have more than 10 years experience you could consider a two-page resume. Additionally, when you are required specify a list of technical and engineering knowledge skills. It is very likely that you should also incorporate some technical information as an addendum or make it available upon request.

If you are at the end of your career, had several board positions, participated in several committees, or are in a very senior or leading position, then the length is no longer an issue considering the track record of the executive. In this case, you could prepare a shorter version and a longer version to be available upon request.

If you are someone involved in scientific, academic, educational or the medical investigation profession instead of using a traditional format of a resume you should considered a Curriculum Vitae or CV. Your academic achievements, courses, thesis, papers, publications, speaking engagements, licenses, patents, etc. are of utmost importance. Also again in this case length is not an issue. You could use addendum sections to allow recruiters to decide whether or not to read the full resume.

In all cases, place the most relevant experiences, skills, and information on the first page. You must captivate the attention of the reader by presenting your credentials up-front, and then you could get into the more detailed information.

Opening Statement

Sometimes it can be useful to include an opening statement (mostly when you are not sending a cover letter). This consists of a brief profile, summary or mission statement where a valued proposition is presented.

This statement can also include your career goals, interests, etc. This may be important when you are planning a change in your career, or when you want to focus the reader on a specific subject on the resume. This also could be an excellent opportunity to present your matching skills.

This statement has to be customized. Do not copy the job description, do not present anything too general, and do not fill with flattery or empty content.

Main Areas of a Resume

Additionally you can split the resume into several areas, taking into consideration the topics most relevant for your experience, industry and objectives, such as:

Name: The full name should at the top of the forefront page of the resume. The font size of the name should be slightly larger than the rest of the text but not much.

Contact Information: Include Address, telephone and e-mail. Usually this is placed at the top of the forefront page of the resume, just below the name in a lower font.

Professional Experience: Include institution name, job title, location, dates, scope of responsibilities, and results. You could also add *internships* (paid and unpaid).

Education or Academic Background: Include institution name, title degree, major, location, dates, honors, and thesis or teaching experience if applicable. Do not include high school or any other basic education if you already have a University degree, except if it is relevant for your prospect employer (prestige, specialization, etc.). Do not include information about GPA unless it is outstanding.

Courses: Include institution name, subject, date, location and sponsors only if it adds value. In some situations avoiding lengthy resumes is important.

Languages: Describe your ability to communicate in other languages. List them and give an idea of your level. For instance: English (native), French (fluent), Spanish (conversational), Italian (basic). If you have courses that support your statements, then it's even better.

Here is an example of a foreign student:

English: Fluent—Level 6/6 (University of California Santa Barbara—UCSB)—Toefl: 673 (2004).

Additional: Include Certifications, Licenses, Awards, Honors, Grants and Fellowships, Speaking engagements, Patents, Affiliations, Community services. The length or distribution of this information will depend on individual experiences. In all cases, you should mention institutions, dates, locations, your functions or roles and any other relevant information.

Sometimes you should add industry skills such as computers skills: Windows XP, Microsoft Office (Word, Excel, Power Point and Outlook), Mind Manager, among others. This section becomes less important with time. If you are a senior executive, the recruiter will assume you have certain skills and you can just skip them.

Some recruiters want to know something more about you. In this section you can include hobbies such as photography, sports, travel, etc. Also add personal qualities (self-motivated, hard working, etc.). Be brief as this information is not too relevant.

Do Not

Do not focus your resume on job duties; instead put the focus on your achievements. Do not use job description to build up your resume. Do not include boring lists of duties without results.

Do not include personal information such as age, marital status, race or physical data (height, weight, etc.). There are however sometimes exceptions to this. For instance if you are applying as a gym instructor the later information could be relevant.

Do not include reasons as to why you left a company in a resume. If appropriate, this information will be asked or disclosed at the interview.

Do not include attachments alongside the resume, such as letters of recommendations, awards, press releases, etc. unless it has been requested. You can present these documents in an interview at a later stage.

Do not overstate past experience. Recruiters are more concerned to know about your latest achievements. The last 10 years are the most relevant.

Do not apply to just any job announcement you find. Read the requirements and the job description. If you do not fulfill the requirements do not send your resume. If for any reason you think that even without fulfilling the requirement you are apt for the job, prepare an outstanding cover letter stating why you think you could meet the job requirements.

Publications: Include the name of the article, book, journal, or paper, and include the publisher or where it was published. Also include the editor, language, location and date. If you belong to a specific industry, follow its standard bibliographic format.

References: They are not necessary at this stage. Employers know that if asked you will present references. In the scientific field, it may be important to include references and to highlight the institutions, job titles, dates, locations, job descriptions, etc. Use the same resources in the entire document.

Time Structure

Remember to always start with the most recent activities and to include previous ones in ***reverse chronological order***.

Point out the most recent or relevant experience first. If you have just started your career you could start with your Academic Background.

However, if you have a ten year work history, it is better to start with your Professional Experience.

Functional Resume

If you are thinking about 1) a radical change of your career, or if you 2) do not have prior experience in the field you are applying to, or 3) if you have date blanks (long periods of unemployment), a functional resume could be your choice.

The structure of a resume is different when using functional resumes. The information is not sorted by date (do not follow a chronological order). Instead, in this case, follow a skill-oriented format. Once you determine which experience is the most relevant to the reader, place it right at the beginning regardless of when you did it. Show the impact on your career of each past job experience and connect your achievements with the job experience.

For instance, you could create a section called "Sales Experience" in which you should list all your past experiences split into Sections: Car Sales, Real Estate Sales, etc, with a summary of your achievements in each one of them

In functional resumes an opening statement can be necessary, such as a strong profile section. Do not use a functional resume except in the three cases mentioned above.

Take Care Of Details

Check for details: Please check grammar, misspelling and formats. Do not forget your contact information including mail, telephone and address. Think ahead. If you are thinking about moving, arrange a permanent address (PO Box, relatives, etc . . .). Who is going to pick up the telephone? Do you have kids? Do you have a maid? How is your greeting on your answering machine? Find an appropriate solution.

Appearance counts. Ask friends and family to review the document thoroughly.

Always Be Truthful

Most job seekers tend to exaggerate accomplishments and lie about their professional experience, fudge dates, titles, etc. One of the main reasons is to disguise the fact that they have been unemployed. This is a shortsighted strategy. In the long run the truth will come out. The benefits are not worth the risk of damaging your reputation. Remember this.

Employers usually do a background check, not only with the contacts you provided as references, but also with other members of the organization, and the human resources department. Any discrepancy will destroy your credibility.

Presentation Format

The standard format is to use letter size paper, a light colored background page and black font. Do not use fancy, strong or multiple colors. Watch out for printing quality, margins, spaces, and other possible small grammatical mistakes in the details.

Should I Include A Picture?

In the US it is not customary to present pictures because of regulations. However, in other countries, depending on the type of job it could be a requirement. In this case glue the picture at the top right corner of the forefront page of the resume or you can uploaded it to your resume. Verify the glue characteristics. The size of the picture should not be too big.

Presentation Letter

What is a Cover Letter?

A cover letter is a one-page letter that summarizes your intentions, qualifications, reinforces your strengths (sales pitch), and proposes a course of action, such as a request for an interview.

The goal is to make the reader pay more attention to you among thousands of candidates. It is your introduction so you have to make a good impression.

It is true that some recruiters do not read them because of lack of time. However, it is extremely important to prepare a cover letter. Human resource staff, headhunters and head of business lines might read the resume directly.

Nevertheless, cover letters are essential for job seekers. It is not simply to write down a few sentences, but quite the opposite. It has to be carefully thought out and must respond to a predefined strategy.

Why Are Presentation Letters Important?

Presentations letters are usually requested because they give the opportunity for the employer to know a little bit more about you. They are important because they show the way you communicate; organize information, your professionalism, clues to your personality, level of commitment and level of perfectionism.

But mostly they are important because they give *you* an additional occasion to reinforce the information you are presenting in your resume, and to gear the reader to conclusions or associations that are important to you. It highlights strengths, skills and experiences most relevant to the reader.

While the resume proposed organized, detailed and structured data in inverse chronological order, the cover letter emphasizes the abilities, skills, strengths and soft data (personality) in a sales pitch paragraph. It reflects how you express yourself. This is why it should be clear and appropriate.

Additionally, the dates, and the names of institutions (except when it is an integral part of your marketing strategy) could be presented following a functional pattern. This means it focuses on your activities or skills, such as sales, business development, investigation, leadership, interpersonal skills, and analytical skills, regardless of time or location.

Before you start writing, analyze the possible needs of your employer and the skills or experiences you have to offer to satisfy the position.

Cover Letter Structure

Normally the letter includes three parts: Opening (reason of the letter or subject), Development (sales pitch) and Closing (next step).

Opening / Subject: Get straight to the point. "I'm writing you to explore current job opportunities at the E-Business Division as Senior Consultant. The purpose of this letter is to express my interest in joining XXX, as YYY" or "I am interested in discussing any entry level positions you might have available"—for recent graduates. You have to help the recruiter do his job by *narrowing the search*. He /she needs to "file" you somehow.

Sometimes you can also include a short description of yourself. "I am a senior SAP programmer", "I have recently graduated with honors from Harvard University". This could be helpful for candidates with specific knowledge or skill set students, or long established professional careers in a single industry. For example, "I'm a senior petrochemical engineer."

Even if you are willing to accept any job, it is important to narrow the search and show that you know what you want. Employers appreciate people with long-term goals for their careers.

Sales Pitch: This is the most creative part. Normally this could be split in two sections. The first section should be a brief description of your career. "I was involved in several areas of investment banking, such as M&A, Private Equity and Fund Management for 6 years in New York and London."

The second section tells why the experience or skills described in the first part makes you the ideal choice for the job. "I believe my experience and my leadership's skills could prove to be valuable for your organization." "I can certainly help you achieve the next stage / growth / objectives, thanks to my proven / broad experience in sales and marketing."

The link between the job description (published or your best assumption) and your skills and experience will guide the reading of your resume. Mention at least *3 to 5 reasons* that make you suitable to obtain the aspired position. Always think what makes you different and special. As an opening statement you could use: "As an economist and former IMF counselor, I can offer the following skills and accomplishments: strong analytical and modeling skills, problem solving mind set and international experience."

Sometimes the skills set you choose to present to the employer can also be presented in a list of bullet points. For example:

- Interpersonal Skills
- Cross Cultural Experience
- Fluent in Japanese

If you are responding to a job posting you could identify, from the job description, the most important skills and experiences requested from the company and use them in the cover letter. Be careful however not to copy the job description. Be smart and creative.

Try to *support statements* with hard data. Do not make empty claims. "I developed a new marketing strategy which resulted in a 45% sales increase." "I was involved in XX Company restructuring, which resulted in 23% cost reduction and 39% gross margin increase".

Next Steps: Propose or suggest next steps. "I would very much appreciate to have the opportunity to meet you", "to arrange a conference call", or "I will be calling you for XX reason." You can contact them with a follow up call.

The overall tone must always be polite, assertive and courteous. Do not show urgency, despair or pressure, and try to take the initiative to follow up.

After the request for action you could also thank the reader and utilize a formal closing, such as: "Sincerely Yours," "Best regards," "Hoping to hear from you soon," and your signature.

Important Issues For Cover Letters

Customization: If you think you will get an interview with a standardized cover letter, you are very likely wrong. Even if you are preparing a massive mailing list, you must set aside some time to tailor make your cover letter. It is important to show interest that is reflected in your knowledge about the company. Invest time on research. Nowadays, the existence of institutional websites allows you to get important information that could be useful for your cover letter. For instance, you will have a better understanding about products, services, activities, corporate structure, geographical coverage, press releases, etc. If you have contacts in the company, then it's even better.

Show your interests: This is called a "flattery statement." Make known that you are aware of future plans, current projects, latest acquisitions, etc. Also make known *why you chose them*. "I've read about the company's ambition to expand internationally and to become a leader in XX market" or "I share that view, goal," etc. "I was very much impressed by the people I met at the launching of XX product." Other areas you could comment on are: "company culture," "reputation," "management philosophy," "mission," "sales or growth track," etc. You must be very well informed.

Addressee: Try to send the letter to a person directly, instead of "to whom it may concern," or "Human Resources," "Careers," etc. Unfortunately, this will not always be possible.

Contact Information: Do not forget to include your telephone numbers (office, cellular, home), address and e-mail.

Negative Information: Never mention conflicts, doubts, sarcasm, etc. Try to avoid negative structures. Instead of "I do not like traveling," replace it with "I enjoy working in XX city." "I am not good at," for "I am better at—the opposite," etc. Prioritize positive sentences.

Compensation Package: Do not mention your desired compensation package except when asked by the employer. If asked however you must include it, otherwise you could be eliminated from the search. Never lie about previous compensations. If you do not feel comfortable stating an exact amount then set a range from XXX to YYY, depending on variable compensation, other benefits, responsibilities, etc. Compensation information should never be presented in your resume. Present it only in a case such as above and only in the cover letter.

Check and recheck: It is of utmost importance not to have grammatical, typos, misspelling or orthographic faults. Make sure several relevant people read the letter. Select only people with "high standards" and that are very "critical." A professional cover letter and resume could place you on a short list. A clean, direct and solid structure is key for success.

Keep Copies: You must have a record of all cover letters sent. If you are called by a recruiter, you should have access to the cover letter sent so you can refer to it to avoid inconsistencies. It is very difficult to remember all interactions; job descriptions for different postings, company information, among other important issues. Make these copies accessible and re-read them before any eventual interview.

Means Of Distribution

The second question is, by which method you will send your contact information and resume to prospective employers. The most common options are:

- **e-mail**
- **Fax**
- **Mail**
- **On-line**

Each one requires different information and strategies.

E-mail: When sending a resume via e-mail, one main question could arise. Should I send the resume and cover letter as an attachment or should it be included in the body of the mail?.

The answer is not straightforward. Some recruiters prefer an attachment, while others prefer to have a quick look at the profile without opening an additional file. Most prefers to read it on paper, therefore the e-mail body gives them the possibility of printing directly from the inbox. Yet others prefer a clean print without the header formats of mails.

Notwithstanding, my recommendation is:

a) Prepare a short presentation in the email body to be used as a hook. You could send the presentation or cover letter as an email body and the resume as an attachment.

b) An attachment in word/pdf is easier to save / file than an e-mail.

c) The formatting is much more appealing in a word processor format that in an e-mail format.

The second most important issue when sending your resume by e-mail is the ***subject***. People are reluctant to open mails from unknown senders due to virus paranoia. There are two approaches that could be used:

a) If your resume is a response to a job offering / advertiser, include in the subject the reference code, for instance RESUME— Reference Search 0453, or RESUME—CFO—Wall Street Journal, etc.

b) If you are sending your resume as your own initiative, include in the subject, the desired position, main function, area, etc. For instance: RESUME—CFO, or RESUME—Emerging Markets, RESUME—Sr. CPA, etc . . .

c) Third, do not forget to attach the file accurately, check for any virus, and do not use strange characters or file formats; otherwise the recipient could have problems reading your mail.

Fax: Usually you must send the cover letter and the resume together. All the other issues remain the same.

Mail: Cover letters and Resumes can be sent in the mail. In this case, the quality of the paper is important. However it is regarded best to avoid regular mail.

On-line Forms: Some employers have their own websites where potential candidates must upload their resumes in a predetermined form. It is easier to expedite the process by having the resume in a word format while uploading the information. By copying and pasting you do not only save time but it also avoids mistakes.

Interactive Phase (II)

This phase is characterized by the interaction with the target employers established in the preparation phase. The interaction could be through letters, e-mails, and telephone or more interestingly through interviews.

Letters: Companies usually send letters when they do not have openings. In these letters they will thank you for your interest in the company, and tell you that your resume has been included in their database for future references. In the short term this is bad news. In the future you never know.

E-mails: You may receive mail with the same content of the letter mentioned above, or you may be asked to conduct a virtual interview. The employer will prepare a set of questions that you will have to answer as part of the recruiting process. Depending of the results of the previous step, you could be asked for a personal interview.

Telephone: Normally if someone calls you it is good news. But be aware that if it is a formal call you should be sharp and ready. If you are not able to speak freely ask the caller when you can reach them at a later time or tell them when will be a good moment to call you back. Be articulate and self-confident (not arrogant). If you are ready to talk, breathe deeply to release tension and start the conference interview. This is always difficult because you cannot see the reaction of the other party.

Interviews: If you reach this level you have completed an important part of your task. You may be on the short list, there could be an opening, or in the worst case scenario your profile was attractive enough to keep you for future references when something does come available. Do not be disappointed. It is good training regardless of whether you get the job or not.

Remember that there are several rounds of interviews, normally going upward in the hierarchical pyramid. You may start in the Human Resources Department and move from middle management to top management. Each interview is like playing an eliminatory game. Bear that in mind.

Please see next chapter to improve interview responsiveness. ***Successful Interviews***

Sometimes pressure and lack of preparation can jeopardize all your efforts. You must be prepared for the interview mentally, professionally and attitudinally.

Get All The Info You Can Get

The more you know about the company, the position and your interviewer the better. You may not be able to show interest for something you do not know. Fortunately, most company websites give you a good idea of their activities, competitive environment, products, services, geographical coverage, press release, etc. If you are applying to a public company (shares traded in a public markets, such as NYSE, NASDAQ, etc.) you may also benefit from viewing annual reports, research from investment banking institutions, etc.

Additionally, if you can get information about the background of the recruiter, areas of interest of the recruiter, job description, reporting line, etc., this could be helpful as well. This information will allow you to prepare yourself better.

It may be a good idea, after getting acquainted with the company, to prepare some questions for the recruiter or to show your interest and knowledge. For instance: What is the expansion strategy? What is the strategy to overcome the highly competitive environment? What is going to be my role in the organization? What expectations does the company have of me (objectives, performance methodology evaluation, etc.)? Of course, these will vary depending on the company and position. Do not ask about a compensation package unless you are asked about your previous compensation package or your expectations.

Be Mentally Prepared

It is extremely common to be nervous. Anxiety is a common reaction, but do not show this to the recruiter. The willingness to do everything right could play against you. To avoid pressure, arrive to the interview a little early, about 15-20 minutes ahead of time, then walk, breath, and think positive. Do not actually show up until the scheduled time.

The only thing you have to do is be yourself. Behave naturally. You have already thought about the interview in advance. Some people like to think about last minute details just before the meeting. Others prefer to read something irrelevant to calm down. Figure out what works best for you.

Big Don'ts

Avoid committing unnecessary mistakes:

- Do not be late
- Do not eat or chew
- Do not show anxiety. Speak slowly.
- Do not look down, as this will not make you appear self-confident. Look to the eyes of the interviewer.
- Do not touch your hair often
- Do not sit back. The best position is to be straight.
- Do not put both elbows on the desk.
- Do not cross your legs or lie back.
- Do not be extremely open and friendly.
- Do not be dubious

Interview Structure

The interview development is normally structured in three stages.

Breaking the Ice: This stage includes salutation and a brief informal set of questions. It is likely that the recruiter will give you a brief description of the company and the objective of the interview. This may include an explanation of the job description.

Presentation: This stage usually starts with the everlasting question; "Well tell me a little bit more about yourself." This is your turn. During this stage, you are the one who speaks the most. You must briefly recapitulate your professional and educational background. It is important to have thought about this stage thoroughly. This is your chance to sell your profile, how you fit with their needs, and how you can add value to the company. Sometimes you need to have flexibility with this speech depending on the job description explained to you in the previous phase. Be articulate, fluent, clear, brief, accurate, and try to make your point whenever it makes sense. Do not oversell. Learn the guidelines of this phase in advance.

Ping Pong: Leave room for some questions. You may have the opportunity to show reflexes, and critical reasoning skills. This could also be the time to ask some questions as well. This interaction is of the utmost importance. When you answer questions be precise about periods, responsibilities, etc. Each question gives you the opportunity to show your skills; so proper argumentation is critical for success.

Be Prepared For Typical Questions

Usually there are several questions that are typical in an interview, such as; where do you see yourself in 5 years? What are your major strengths and weaknesses? Are you more prone to be proactive or reactive? And the list goes on. Other questions could be based on explaining changes in your career or why you left a company or were terminated from it.

You must be prepared, but do not try to memorize the answers. You must know the "story," or the big picture. You have to sound articulate and natural. Unfortunately, most people lie in interviews and recruiters are less likely to "believe" if you sound like you are acting. Your credibility could fade away. Take your time to answer and do not hurry even if the answer is obvious to you. The SWOT analysis mentioned before could prove to be very helpful. You must know your aptitudes. Reinforce your answers with background experiences and hard data.

Be Prepared For Anything

Some of the questions can be predictable and some not so predictable. Some recruiters, mostly in long processes when more than 6 people interview you, use one of the interviews to test your resistance for pressure and tend to be very rude. Sometimes, in certain countries, you might be filmed or watched when left alone in a room. Some do not even look at you and treat you poorly. In those cases be polite, but firm. Saying something like, "Excuse me, perhaps this is not the right time for you, we can reschedule the meeting some other time." These processes were quite common in investment banking.

Do Not Give Up Too Much Information

Sometimes when applying for a job, people have their own agenda. As some companies pay for MBAs, courses, etc you may want to benefit from them. However do not mention this as one of the reasons for applying to the position. Sometimes, you also have personal reasons for applying to a certain job, such as relocation, family pressures, etc. If you had conflicts with previous bosses or institutions, when asked, limit the scope of the answer by responding, we do not share the same strategy, goals, tactics, etc.

Learn While You Go

During the interview process you will be told things about the company, and you will get to know the character of the recruiters. Be smart, listen!. Learn from what you are hearing and apply it in your answers or comments. It is also important to figure out the level of formality of the interview. Do not be extremely friendly.

Keep Your Concentration

Interviews usually take between 30 to 60 minutes. If you feel you are losing concentration, breathe regularly and deep, look to the recruiter in the eyes and relax. This is just another human being doing his/her job.

Some psychological tests prove that if you look at facial gestures pleasing to you, this can actually reduce tension. It may work for you.

Arrange A Follow Up

Before leaving the interview make sure to clarify if you will be contacted by them or vice versa. Either way it is not a bad idea to call or send a thank you e-mail after the interview., Also perhaps send another email in a couple of weeks to touch base and show continued interest about the company and the position to which you are applying.

Other Types Of Interviews

The hiring process is costly. Companies place great importance in hiring people for the long run. This is why they try to infuse logic and predictability into hiring. Interviews, reference checks, personality tests, etc. have only one objective, to pick the right candidate.

In the past, job descriptions, duties and responsibilities were more standard. The functional organization was more static and everybody knew what to expect from each position. Nowadays new organizational forms such as alliances, joint ventures, post M&A institutions, less hierarchical structures, dual reporting (business line, geographical line), existence of free agents, international team coordination requirements, etc. make the selection process very difficult and complex. It is becoming an art instead of a science.

Job description tends to be "desired skills", not "possible skills". Some job descriptions are even contradictory. "We want someone aggressive, but conservative." It is impossible to have all the desired components in one single person. It is far more feasible to form a team of people with different skill sets that as a whole bring balance to the company.

A different set of interviews could take place. For instance, you could be involved in a series of group activities to show your leadership skills, team spirit, etc. Sometimes you may be asked to submit tests, IQ (intellectual coefficient) tests, psychological tests, and even astrological tests.

There is not much you can do about the latter tests. However, during group activities, try to participate, articulate your arguments properly and do not be too aggressive. Listen to others and try to assume a genuine leadership position. Remember it is not about talking in a substantive way, but saying things that make a lot of sense and demonstrate good judgment. Make your point clear. Do not overuse first person speech since it tends to create distance. It is better to reach a consensus.

Passive Phase (III)

This is the most difficult phase because it is not in your hands. You are waiting for someone to call you, or to receive news from the people you have contacted. Yet you will soon find out, that your timings are not exactly your prospect employer's timing. Waiting for a potential call is your main priority, but for the companies you have applied for a job, it is only one more assignment to do.

Control Anxiety

Controlling anxiety is key, though honestly difficult. Try to be busy and don't wait beside the phone or check e-mail each ten minutes. Forget about it. If you have been selected they will leave you a message any way.

Follow Up System

It is important to have a perfect record of all contacts with potential employers. You could create a database with the name of the company and the dates you have contacted them (or vice versa). It is important to make sure who has established contact. Always write down the next step, i.e. "they will call me in a week", etc . . . Eliminate the ones you had received negative responses from.

There are several ways of doing this. You could just create a spreadsheet or you could use some CRM (Customer Relationship Manager) software you find on-line. Use whatever works best for you, but always have a follow up system. The bottom line is to be organized and to be aware of the next steps.

Calculate the probabilities of all prospective jobs depending on feedback, follow up, intuition, and other factors. Put more effort toward the ones with higher probabilities.

Be Focused, Alert, Informed, Prompt and Patient

"Attitude is a very little thing that makes a big difference." Never forget that.

Be focused: You should have priorities. Attack the jobs you most want in order of priorities. Some people when unemployed are less focused because they do not manage their time appropriately. Set goals for yourself and accomplish them. For instance, "Today I will prepare presentations to X, Y, Z companies (Resume, Presentation Letters) and mail them."

Be alert: Every interaction you have could give you a piece of information you need. When having social events listen to people. You may become aware of a new division being created in a company, or that a friend has just been appointed to a new company. You never know.

Be informed: Read newspapers, business magazines, listen to the news, etc. The information you gather could be helpful in a potential interview, or it could give you hints about where to look for a job. Additionally this information could be used in a presentation letter.

Be prompt: When facing an opportunity you have to react quickly. You must have the marketing material ready to be customized when something shows up. If you have a new idea, do not take time to work on it. It could fade away quickly.

Be patient: Once you send your resume out, you will become anxious for an answer. Do not be. These processes take time. If you start to get desperate you will only commit mistakes.

Compensation Packages

Most all negotiations will include the following components.

Salary: The annual base salary continues to be the most important component in the negotiation with the new employer. Sometimes, financially, the variable compensation package could be more attractive than the fixed compensation. However, the fixed component is what will determine your "life style". It is never wise to use variable compensation to cover fixed expenses.

Insurance: Most corporate employers offer their employees health, dental and life insurance. Usually, the larger the company the better the benefit package offered.

Pension Plan: Pension plans provide retirement income to employees built from employer and/or employee contributions. In most countries the contribution by the company to the employee's pension is mandatory; in some others it is optional. Very large corporations establish their own pension fund system.

Variable Compensation:

Many companies have initiated new compensation packages, where variable compensation has become increasingly important. This trend is spreading. Companies are more willing to share their benefits rather than being locked into high fixed commitments (burn rate of the head count).

Bonus: A bonus is an additional payment on top of your salary that represents a compensation for your performance. Each position has an associated bonus. A bonus is normally at the discretion of the company.

Sometimes, even if you have done a fantastic job individually, if your division or the company as a whole has performed poorly, it can sabotage your bonus.

Most intermediate management positions have an associated bonus equivalent to one to four monthly salaries.

Guaranteed Bonus: For top producers or executives, when changing jobs, some companies offer a guaranteed bonus. This is normally paid in one to three annual installments.

Signing or Joining Bonus: This is an incentive to join the new company when you have a secure position in your current company, you have a client base, you are being relocated, you have "earned" a compensation but have not been paid yet, or when you are an exceptional employee/ executive. There are other reasons but these are the most important ones.

Revenue / Profit Sharing Agreements: For positions with strong P&L liaisons, another type of variable compensation is revenue or profit sharing agreements. In this case, there is a contract where the company recognizes a percentage of the gross/net income generated by the employee or the division he manages.

Stock Options: This is a more complex instrument. Stock options give you the option of acquiring shares in the company at a known price in the future (strike or base price) and at a preset date (expiration, exercise date). The strike price is usually below that of the market or valuation price, which gives employees the opportunity to generate a capital gain. On the other hand you are very unlikely able to sell these shares freely. A vesting period from 3 to 5 years is normally set. Otherwise the employees could cash in the capital gain and leave the company.

The main objective of this kind of compensation is to increase the loyalty of employees and diminish company turnover. Secondly, it represents a mechanism to lower the salaries paid (less fixed cost) and to share the risk of the venture / company with its employees.

Theoretically this process is very interesting because it allows employees to capture the added value they are generating.

In practice you have to be aware of the real value of these stock options. If the company shares are quoted on a public market (NYSE, NASDAQ, etc), you will have a good idea of how much you are receiving. Additionally the liquidity is guaranteed. However, if the company is not public (is privately held), you will not have liquidity unless the company goes public or gets sold (cash out). In this case the value of the stock option package is less attractive. Moreover, you will not have a clear idea whether the strike valuation is too high or too low except by the information you get from the company itself.

Relocation Package: A relocation package is usually used when one employee is hired or transferred from one location to another. Most companies will pay for moving expenses plus travel expenses for the employee and their direct family members.

Expatriate Package: The "ex-pat" packages include the relocation package plus other benefits. The most important component is the payment of most living expenses including rent, car, private school, etc. It is also common to have an established number of trips to the "home" country, not only for the employee but also for their direct family members. This type of compensation is usually found in middle to top management positions only.

All these compensation packages can be presented on the negotiation table. The more aware you are the better outcome you might have.

My Personal Experience

When I became unemployed (2001) I was a ten-year experienced executive. My career could be divided in three main sectors: three years as a macroeconomic consultant, six years in investment banking and two years in the Internet industry.

In the year 2000, I was the COO of a leading European Internet company where I had to expand the company internationally, which was key to launching the company public (IPO Initial Public Offering). We closed a first financing round of approximately USD 53 Million. However when the Internet market started to melt down, we were involved in a road show for the second round of financing. As the valuation and the chances of raising more money were slim, all international expansion was called off.

I had to fire several people, and I was terminated as well. At that point, I had just been relocated to a country where I did not want to be. I had a six-month rental contract I could not get rid of easily. I decided it was not a good time to start looking for a job because it was going to be extremely difficult being away from target markets (Europe or US), due to the relocation mentioned before.

I was very concerned about being away from the labor market for a long time. I had to do something to fill the unemployment gap in my resume. I thought about obtaining a MBA to expand my job scope (I have a Master degree in Economics). But that was going to take a long time and the enrolment period was over.

Finally, I came up with the idea of writing a book about all that I learned from Internet Business Ventures. This allowed me to accomplish several goals simultaneously. First of all, I was producing an intangible value, investing in me. Secondly, as I asked twenty companies to present their cases, I was still in the market and growing my network by contacting top executives on a daily basis. Third, the book gave me an extra exit strategy as a consultant. In fact, I was hired by six companies to help them redefine their business models; prepare their business plan or due diligence package; coordinate fundraising road shows; develop expansion strategies and design a downsizing plan.

My main goal was turning my previous experience in the Internet industry into a success story instead of a failure.

Of course, the process was not easy. I did not know if I was going to find a publisher. I spent almost nine months (much more than I thought) researching and writing. When I received the news that McGraw-Hill (my first choice), was publishing my book. I could not be prouder! Then the publishing process took an extra three months including the web site, and CD-Rom development.

At the same time I set up my own consulting company focus on three different areas of interest: Internet, Asset Management and Real Estate. This allowed me to reduce my depression from being out of the market and also to have a positive cash flow.

Meanwhile, I moved back to a friendlier market to try to find a new job (United States). Once I had finished the hard part of the book, I thoroughly researched how to write cover letters, resumes, etc. and how to prepare my marketing materials. I waited until the launch of the book to have extra media exposure. I also wanted to have the book ready to give it to prospective employers, so it could be used as supporting promotional material.

As a distribution strategy, I chose to start a one-to-many at the beginning through Head Hunters, and Internet based search firms to maximize the reach. Then, I deployed a one-to-one strategy based on prospective industries. I told friends, contacts and referrals that I was in the market and forwarded my resume just in case. I increased my social life by doing sports, which allowed me to reduce stress and improve relationships.

As I was able to apply to at least three industries (Banking, Internet and Consulting), I prepared three different resumes and cover letters based on my SWOT analysis. Then I acquired a list of companies in target markets, and prepared customizing letters to the CEOs, Managing Partners and Brand Managers depending on the industry.

The results from the Headhunters and Internet based firms were disappointing but predictable considering market environment. Personal contacts helped me a great deal.

I reviewed web sites, read press releases, and researched reports of public companies to be fully prepared for interviews. I started the interview process. There was not much happening in the market, but failure was not an option.

Thanks to a consulting job I did for an Internet base company, I was referred to a new client that asked me to help set up a real estate fund in the US to acquire properties within the US. This led me to know my current employer.

After several months working in the real estate industry, I was finally offered a very interesting position as Director of Operations and Finance, with the main objective to lead the expansion of one of the most respected real estate companies in Florida.

Final Remarks

Unemployment is one of the most stressful experiences in one's life and one of today's most widespread afflictions.

Take the opportunity to do things that you had been unable to do before due to a lack of time during your unemployment period.

Take the search process seriously. There is a lot of competition out there. But if you follow the tips given in the cover letter, resume and interview sections, you will have a much better chance to succeed.

Finally, take proactive steps to narrow down your problems. Redefine your budget and portfolio in a timely manner it could save you a great deal of concern. Increase communication with your loved ones, and do your best to keep your family united. At the end of the day, family is the most important thing you have.

Always look ahead and embrace change.

The future could be a better place to be.

I wish you all the best and good luck!!!

About the Author

Mr. Albert is the Director of Operations & Finances of a vertically integrated real estate group in South Florida, with interests in the areas of Developments, Exclusive Sales & Marketing and Brokerage, with a sales volume over $3 Billon per year. Before, he acted as COO for Latin America for the largest Internet Incubator firm in Spain, which had 8 portfolio companies in Europe, USA and Latin America. In 2001, McGraw-Hill Professional published his book called "Internet Business Models—a post crisis vision". Prior to Internet, he worked as an investment banker for top international banks in New York, London, Paris, Madrid, Geneva and Buenos Aires. He has a BA & MS in Economics; he graduated with honors "Magna Cum Laude". Finally, Albert has performed public speaking engagements in over 20 countries, wrote several articles and has had a strong coverage in press, radio and TV including a CNN live interview.